MW01616581

TEXAS TECH

RED RAIDER FOOTBALL LEGENDS

By
John Henry

GREAT TEXAS LINE PRESS

Texas Tech
Red Raider Football Legends

Editor and book designer: Tom Johanningmeier
Cover designer: Cynthia Wahl
Cover photos by: Darren Carroll
Illustrator: Timberlan Pikes

ISBN: 978-1-892588-623

For bulk sales and whole inquiries contact:

Great Texas Line Press
Post Office Box 11105
Fort Worth, TX 76110
greattexas@hotmail.com
817-922-8929
To see our complete list of Texas guide, humor and cook
books, visit: www.greattexasline.com

Great Texas Line Press strives to be socially responsible, donating
a portion of proceeds from several books to Habitat for Humanity
of Fort Worth, North Fort Worth Historical Society, Texas Dance
Hall Preservation Inc. and Terlingua's Big Bend Educational Foundation. Hundreds of books are donated annually to public-radio
stations throughout Texas for fundraising. Every effort is made to
engage Texas writers, editors, illustrators, designers and photog-
raphers affected by the newspaper industry crisis.

Contents

In the Beginning

AFTER MUCH AGITATION, Gov. Pat Neff signed Senate Bill 103 in 1923, creating Texas Technological College, what would be renamed Texas Tech University and become largest comprehensive higher education institution in the western two-thirds of the state.

The Red Raiders are all grown up, actually centenarians.

Football was at the top of the list of things to do when word reached the High Plains about the new university.

The university hired veteran coach E.Y. Freeland to start the program. He had coached at (now defunct) Daniel Baker College in Brownwood, Austin College in Sherman, TCU in Fort Worth and SMU in Dallas.

Wearing scarlet and black, the Tech "Matadors" took the field – actually the South Plains Fairgrounds – to play Abilene's McMurry College, also founded in 1923. Freeland's wife had suggested the Matador nickname, noting the Spanish Renaissance architecture of the early campus buildings. He reportedly selected the colors and was the first to use the iconic Double T.

Before a crowd of 5,000, the inaugural 1925 gridiron matchup ended in an anticlimactic 0-0 tie.

A latter-day coach, Mike Leach, would have been beside himself.

But that was the beginning of football at Tech, which would nurture enduring traditions that students and alumni hold dear.

Five years later, Pete Cawthon would take the reins.

Around 1935, a *Lubbock Avalanche-Journal* reporter began calling the football team the "Red Raiders," what with the Matadors in their flashy uniforms going across the Midwest "raiding the country" from the South Plains.

But the Matador nickname found a swift end in a Mexican border town.

"During that season Pete took his boys across the border after a game to see Juarez, Mexico," according to *Tender Tyrant: The Legend of Pete Caw-*

thon. A bullfight was included in the itinerary, a sporting if bloody spectacle few of the players had ever seen.

About halfway through the program, Cawthorn staggered out of the Plaza de Toros, white-faced and sick.

"I don't want you boys ever to be called 'Matadors' again," the book recounted. "We've got to get a new name."

That day he changed the name to Red Devils, though Cawthorn reportedly never liked it much himself. But the moniker the *A-J* had used caught his eye.

Texas Tech would be the Red Raiders.

With it a great tradition was born.

Elmer Tarbox

ELMER TARBOX ARRIVED ON CAMPUS never having played a single game of football, let alone a down. He excelled as an athlete in Higgins, a small Panhandle community on the Oklahoma border, but the high school was too small to field a gridiron team.

Somehow spotting untested talent, Cawthorn picked Tarbox out of a crowd one day and urged him to join the Red Raiders. Tarbox had been stopping by to watch the daily practices, intrigued by the game.

That serendipitous start triggered a storied collegiate sports career that ended in glory with the "Higgins Hurricane" selected the Cotton Bowl's most outstanding player in the 1939 game, although it was a 20-13 loss to the Galloping Gaels of St. Mary's. The distinction was accompanied by an offer to turn pro.

During his three seasons of play at Tech, 1936-38, Tarbox became one of the country's best two-way players. As a senior, he was named All-American honorable mention as a halfback after leading the country in yards per catch while finishing seventh in the nation in rushing yards and 10th for receiving yards.

As a defender, Tarbox set the team's single-season record with 11 interceptions, a mark that has never been seriously. It had taken more than five decades for his 17-career interceptions to be eclipsed by Tracy Saul.

Elmer the Great went on to be drafted by the Cleveland Rams of the NFL, the second Red Raider to be selected by the league. Tarbox went 18th overall in 1939, but he didn't play a minute, opting instead to enlist, earning his wings in the U.S. Army Air Corps. As a pilot, he flew with Gen. Claire Lee Chennault's Flying Tigers in the India-China-Burma Theater during World War II. For his service, Tarbox was awarded an Air Medal, a Silver Star, a Purple Heart, and China's Golden Eagle, which was presented by the Chinese Nationalist leader, Generalissimo Chiang Kai-shek. Tarbox later served in the Texas State House.

The Border Conference

TEXAS TECH WAS NEVER SHY about its keen desire to join the Southwest Conference, considered the elite athletic consortium in Texas. But for many years, the feeling wasn't mutual.

The Border Conference was founded in 1931 with charter members Arizona, Northern Arizona, Arizona State, New Mexico, and New Mexico State.

Texas Tech was admitted in 1932. Texas Western, Hardin-Simmons, and West Texas Teachers College would later join.

Tech was the dominant football program, winning nine championships in its almost 25 years in the conference.

The Southwest Conference

THE DREAM OF ALMOST 30 YEARS, carefully nurtured, as the *Lubbock Avalanche-Journal* reported, "and given tender, loving care, blossomed into fruition" when Tech was finally asked in May 1956 to become the eighth member of the Southwest Conference.

"It is the express intention of the conference to admit Texas Tech to its membership as soon as satisfactory arrangement of the details can be concluded," said a statement by the conference, which had not added a new team since 1922, when TCU joined.

"We appreciate the support and cooperation of everybody in Lubbock, in West Texas and all of Texas," said coach DeWitt Weaver. "We're going to do everything in our power to make Texas Tech a worthy member of the conference."

Saddle up, Tramps

BOLSTERING RED RAIDER TRADITIONS are the Saddle Tramps, who have been loudly ubiquitous on game day since the spirit group's founding in 1936.

The all-male Tramps lead cheers, organize and participate in pep rallies, and generally foster school pride on campus, in the community and at other athletic events. They also are involved in co-ordinating tailgate parties and assisting with other game-day operations. And the Tramps serve as the honor guard for the Masked Rider before games.

The Masked Rider

IN 1954, COACH DEWITT WEAVER told head cheerleader Joe Kirk Fulton that Tech needed a live mascot. Fulton and others brainstormed and came up with the Masked Rider.

As an experienced horseman, Fulton was asked to be the inaugural Masked Rider New Year's Day 1954 at the Gator Bowl. Fulton galloped around the stadium to an awe-struck crowd on a black horse named Blackie.

"No team in any bowl game ever made a more sensational entrance," the *Atlanta Journal-Constitution* commented.

A statue of Fulton on his steed graces the grounds of the Frazier Pavilion at Texas Tech University.

Since that first season, the rider – both male and female – has led the football team onto the field before each home game, and the iconic entrance is accompanied by the university's fight song, *Fight, Raiders, Fight*.

Will Rogers and Soapsuds

RIDING INTO THE SUNSET, a statue of humorist-commentator Will Rogers astride horse Soapsuds, was given to the university by newspaper publisher Amon G. Carter, a close friend of Rogers' who had commissioned Electra Waggoner Biggs to create it two years after the famous Oklahoman's death in 1935. Three identical statues were given to Fort Worth, Dallas and Claremore, Oklahoma.

According to Tech lore, it's no accident that Soapsuds' posterior faces the direction of College Station, home of rival Texas A&M.

In any event, Soapsuds has become ingrained in the campus football tradition.

The night before every home game, the Saddle Tramps wrap up Will and Soapsuds with red crepe paper.

The story handed down maintains that the Saddle Tramps jumped to action after finding Soapsuds covered in maroon paint after a Tech victory over the Aggies in 1969.

The Voice

JACK DALE DIDN'T ATTEND Texas Tech. He didn't even go to college.

But for 50 years Jack Dale was the voice of Red Raiders football and men's basketball.

"I think he was a big-time talent in a smaller market and probably somewhere along the line could have moved on somewhere else," John Harris, a color analyst on Tech football broadcasts since 1982, told the *Avalanche-Journal*. "But I think he loved doing what he was doing at Texas Tech, and I think he was loyal to the people who gave him a chance, and I think Texas Tech was better off for it."

Growing up in Alma, Kansas, Dale dreamed of being a sportscaster. He called imaginary games to himself as a farmboy driving a tractor. After six months at a Kansas City's Pathfinder School of Radio Announcing, he sent letters to 113 stations in the fall of 1952.

He was hired for a job in Lubbock.

"Listen, I'm telling you, all this was ordained," Dale told the *A-J* in 2002. "It was ordained for me to come to KFYO in Lubbock. I sent them a tape of a game that I did in Topeka, Kansas, that had to be the worst portrayal of a football game that anybody had ever done or anybody had ever listened to."

Dale was inducted in the Texas Sports Hall of Fame in 2005. He died six years later.

'The Beast'

IT WAS SAID MORE THAN ONCE, that E.J. Holub was a cowboy who liked to play football.

He embodied the larger-than-life West Texan, a tall, lean rancher in Wranglers, topped with a cowboy hat and punch crease.

"The Beast," born in Schulenburg and raised in Lubbock, was a two-time All-America center under DeWitt Weaver from 1959-60, the school's so-called "bridge years" when it transitioned from the Border Conference to the Southwest. They weren't particularly historic years for the team, but Holub would become Texas Tech's first member of the College Football Hall of Fame.

He impacted games from both sides of the ball.

"I played against that guy in high school and when you try to block him it's like trying to block a tree," recalled Glynn Gregory, who played for SMU and before that at Abilene High School.

Holub gathered up a whole bunch of firsts at Tech. He was the first in school history to earn

All-America honors twice in a career. He was also Tech's first consensus All-American as a senior in 1960 as well as the school's first selection to the All-SWC team the same year.

E.J. Holub

As a senior, Holub finished 10th in the Heisman Trophy voting.

Against Baylor that year, he had 15 unassisted tackles and eight assists. Later against Arkansas, he harassed the Razorbacks with 18 unassisted tackles and assisted on 10 others

During his stellar 1960 season, *Sports Illustrated* named him Lineman of the Week following a performance against Baylor that saw him make 15 unassisted tackles and assist on eight others. That same year, against Arkansas, the 6-4, 215-pound Holub had 18 unassisted tackles, assisted on 10 others, and intercepted a pass and returned it 40 yards for Tech's only score against the seventh-ranked team.

So impressive was this lineman that the city of Lubbock celebrated "E.J. Holub Day" after the game, his last as a college player.

His best playing days were ahead, of course.

Holub, noted for his fiery disposition on the field, was drafted high by both the Dallas Cowboys of the NFL and the Dallas Texans of the AFL. He chose to go the way of the AFL and Lamar Hunt, who eventually moved the team to Kansas City and changed the name to the Chiefs.

Holub started 113 games for the Texans and Chiefs over nine years. He is distinguished as the only player to start on both offense and defense in the history of the Super Bowl.

In Super Bowl I, he started at linebacker. He was the starting center in the Chiefs' Super Bowl IV appearance.

In every season from 1961 to 1966, Holub was either an AFL All-Star or first-team All-AFL selection. In 1963, he tied for the most interceptions by a linebacker with five. He'd go on to finish his career as a three-time AFL champion and Super Bowl winner when the Chiefs took a flyswatter to the Vikings in Super Bowl IV in New Orleans.

Holub is one of eight players in Tech's Ring of Honor at AT&T Jones Stadium, and was the first in school history to have his number, No. 55, retired.

"When you think of the prestige of what it means to be in the Ring of Honor, you quickly think of E.J. Holub," Former Tech player and coach Rodney Allison told the *Lubbock Avalanche-Journal*.

Holub retired after the 1971 season, his knees looking, he said, as if "they lost a knife fight with a midget."

Years later, *Avalanche-Journal* writer Don Williams recalled seeing the living legend at the annual Texas Tech Hall of Fame induction banquet, generally held the night before Tech hosted A&M or Texas.

"What are we going to do tomorrow, E.J.?" the emcee asked playfully.

"Kick their ass!" Holub shouted to an approving guest list.

Trailblazer

IN 1966, TEXAS TECH doggedly recruited Fort Worth basketball player James Cash, the I.M. Terrell star coached by Robert Hughes. Deciding between Tech and TCU, Cash ultimately decided he wanted to stay close to home.

So, it was Danny Hardaway of Lawton, Oklahoma, who made history in 1967 as the first African-American to receive an athletic scholarship to Texas Tech, picking the Red Raiders over 37 other offers for football, including Oklahoma, in addition to 10 for basketball, including UCLA and coach John Wooden.

He was following in the footsteps of other trailblazers.

Six years prior, Lucille Sugar Barton Graves became the first Black student admitted to Texas Tech. In 1964, Ophelia Powell-Malone, a transfer from Huston-Tillotson College, became the first Black student to receive a bachelor's degree at the university. In 1965, Stella Courtney Crockett was the first African-American student to complete all four years of undergraduate study at the school and earn a bachelor's degree.

Hardaway told the *Avalanche-Journal*: "When I had the opportunity to come to Tech, I was really honored that they thought I was the guy to do it,"

Hardaway, 6-foot-3, 205 pounds, proved a good fit in two seasons for the Red Raiders, gaining 794 yards rushing in 1969-70 combined, as well as 265 yards receiving and four total touchdowns. But he transferred to Cameron University in his hometown of Lawton, Oklahoma, for his senior season.

The Golden Palomino

DONNY ANDERSON WAS ONCE believed to be a baseball prospect who might merit a big signing bonus. "I quit thinking about baseball after I hit .204 last year," he said in 1965, his senior season at Texas Tech.

Football is what made No. 44, all 6-foot-3, 210 pounds of him, a Tech legend forever known as "The Golden Palomino," a slicing, long-striding runner with size and speed, and eventual College Football Hall of Fame member.

"Doak [Walker] could do so many things," Texas Tech coach J.T. King said. "You'd stop his running and he'd beat you with his receiving. "Donny is the same way."

SMU coach Hayden Fry called Anderson "the most complete football player in America."

Tech fans who were around remember the 1965 season as simply magical.

The team went 8-2 with a Gator Bowl appearance. Anderson as its "Merlin" was one of the best players in the country, just as Fry had said. *The*

Donny Anderson

Sporting News thought so too, naming him Co-Player of the Year, with Jim Grabowski of Illinois.

Anderson ran back a kickoff 100 yards against Oklahoma State, caught 10 passes against Arkansas, and scored 17 touchdowns that season. As a junior, Anderson led the country in all-purpose yards with more than 1,700. Anderson closed with 5,111, a Texas Tech yardage record.

Anderson could have turned pro his junior year, but decided to stay another year despite the Green Bay Packers having picked him in the first round of the 1965 draft.

The game against Texas A&M in Lubbock stands out in a season of singular memories.

Anderson had been held for 21 yards rushing in the first half, but he beat the Aggies as a receiver, scoring on a swing pass, which he hauled in, ran over a would-be tackling linebacker and then scampered 8 yards for a touchdown.

That was small potatoes compared with what was to come.

Trailing the Aggies with a minute, 18 seconds left in the game, the Raiders got cute in the huddle. On the next play, quarterback Tom Wilson found a curling Jerry Shipley, who caught the pass and then promptly tossed a lateral to Anderson, who saw "nothing but daylight."

Anderson scored with 31 seconds left to shock the Reveilles.

Anderson had told Shipley to look for him after catching Wilson's pass.

"I'll be close. Toss me a lateral," he said.

Few players ever received more fanfare upon entering the NFL than did Anderson, nicknamed one of the "Gold Dust Twins." He and Grabowski signed rookie contracts for a combined $1 million.

Anderson signed for an unprecedented $700,000 with the Packers, eclipsing the $400,000 the New York Jets paid Joe Namath. That's a whopping $6.5 million in 2023 dollars. (Yeah, chump change by modern-day standards.)

Green Bay would be cold, but at least he could

afford the heating bill.

It was anticipated that he would replace Paul Hornung at halfback.

One of his best games was the renowned Ice Bowl against the Dallas Cowboys, considered among the most famous games in NFL history. With the temperature at minus-13 (minus-48 with wind chill), Anderson handled the ball 30 times, including punts, and shined in the 68-yard final drive by catching three passes for 27 yards. He also picked up two pivotal first downs.

His totals were pedestrian in the brutal conditions: 79 total yards. He also punted eight times for 230 yards.

Afterward, Vince Lombardi, the Packers coach, embraced his rookie: "You became a man today. I'm really proud of you."

In six seasons with Green Bay, Anderson never met the sky-high expectations, yet he never missed a game and led the Packers in rushing in 1968 and 1970. Two weeks after his clutch performance in the Ice Bowl, Anderson had a touchdown and 66 yards from scrimmage in the Packers' victory over Oakland in Super Bowl II.

Señor Sack

TYREE WILSON, A MEMBER of the 2022 Tech team and a first-round draft pick by the Las Vegas Raiders, has entered the conversation as the school's best defensive lineman. Cases can be made for others.

None, however, to this point, is Señor Sack, a.k.a. Gabe Rivera, who lived life in triumph and terrible tragedy.

Rivera, who was born in the Valley town of Crystal City, was a standout two-way player – a tight end and linebacker – at San Antonio Jefferson High School. As a senior, he was selected to the prestigious Parade All-American team.

Colleges salivated. He was said to have had 15 serious suitors, including Notre Dame, Arizona and Baylor.

Many were taken by surprise when Rivera chose Texas Tech, which he appeared to use as a platform for greatness as a professional football player.

Gabe Rivera

"We started hearing about this big, huge guy coming in," remembered quarterback Ron Reeves. "He shows up at camp and gets going, and just the excitement of having somebody that big, that strong, that fast. ... Even though he was from San Antonio, he just was simple. He didn't come in with a big ego. He just came in to be one of the boys and did a great job of fitting in."

The Red Raiders weren't very good over Rivera's four seasons, managing a 13-28-3 record, but he was honorable mention All-American as a sophomore and Southwest Conference defensive player of the year and consensus All-American as a senior.

His 321 career tackles included a team-high 105 in 1982 and 14 career sacks. He was named to the SWC all-decade team for the 1980s.

Rivera cemented his status as a top NFL prospect during a game against No. 1 Washington his senior season. The Red Raiders had a mediocre 3-3 record. The Huskies, at 6-0, had been averaging 40 points a game and, playing at home, were forecast to blow out the visitors.

Don't uncork the champagne prematurely.

Led by Rivera, the Raiders held the Huskies to 10 points in a loss.

"Gabe was like a mad hornet trapped in a fast-moving car with all the windows up," the *Avalanche-Journal*'s Norval Pollard wrote. "The Huskies didn't know whether to pull over, open all the doors, and wait until he escaped or keep traveling and hope he stayed at the rear window."

Washington coach Don James called Rivera "best defensive player I've seen."

The Pittsburgh Steelers passed on quarterback Dan Marino, instead grabbing Rivera with the 21st pick in the 1983 NFL Draft.

Then tragedy struck.

In October, seven games into his rookie season, Rivera was legally intoxicated when he crashed his Datsun 280ZX into another car in a violent collision. Rivera was ejected through the rear window. He suffered head, neck, chest and abdominal injuries that left him a paraplegic.

He never walked again.

"He was just the most outstanding athlete that I was ever blessed to coach, and I coached a lot of awful good ones." said Dean Slayton, Rivera's position coach at Tech. "But Gabe was exceptional.

"He was destined, I believe, to be one of the best defensive linemen that the pro football league had ever really seen. There are great ones there now and have been in the past, but I think he would have been one of those."

Rivera died in 2018 at 57.

Mighty Mite Can-Do

TYRONE THURMAN WAS FIRST-TEAM All-American as a kick returner in 1988. He was all-conference in 1986 and '88, the same year he led his team in pass receiving with 48 receptions for 726 yards and four touchdowns. He set a school record for punt return average at 13.5 yards in 1985.

And he did it all at *5-foot-4ish* and 145 pounds.

Tyrone Thurman

This mightiest of mighty mites proved that short people have all sorts of reasons to excel, especially if they can run.

Oh, and he also played 13 games for the *basketball* team in 1989.

The multi-purpose threat also was a special teams star, returning four punt returns for scores,

31

including a school-record 96-yard return against Texas in 1986.

"My job was the easiest thing," Thurman liked to say, in his genuinely humble way. "My job was just to catch the ball and run the ball. The hardest job out there are the guys blocking, holding their blocks and doing their grunt work."

Thurman also set school records for most return yards in a season with 444 in 1986, returns in a career with 126, and return yards in a career with 1,466.

As a receiver, he finished his college career with 93 receptions for 1,270 yards and five receiving TDs. After college, he had a stint with the Dallas Cowboys and then played two seasons in the Canadian Football League and five seasons in the Arena Football League.

Goooaaal!

TEXAS TECH SHUT OUT Texas A&M 12-0 at home in 2001, but the fireworks occurred afterward.

Chaos and *disorder* are actually more suitable words.

A zealous student section charged the field and tore down the goal post, a not so atypical act by celebrating college football fans. However, the throng wasn't satisfied.

The students picked up the goal post and began marching it to the Aggies section of the stadium.

When they got there, none other than Dr. Mike McKinney – Texas Gov. Rick Perry's chief of staff – was waiting.

A fight ensued involving McKinney, whose son Seth was a member of the Aggies football team. The medical doctor-turned-politician left the stadium with a black eye and eight stitches.

"I pushed two of them down and grabbed my binoculars and said, 'The next one that comes up gets it,'" McKinney told the A&M campus newspaper, *The Battalion*. "Then somebody who was already in the stands, I guess, came up and knocked the fool out of me. I saw him hit me – a kid in a red shirt."

Only it wasn't a kid in a red shirt. According to Tech President David Schmidly, the assailant was an *A&M* student. And there was film footage to confirm it.

Kliff, the Favorite Son

IN 2023, THE UNIVERSITY announced that it would induct Kliff Kingsbury into its football Ring of Honor. Kliff was the first to be given the keys to Mike Leach's high-octane, weird, wild offense. His senior season was tantamount to a room of loosened up slot machines hitting all winners at the same time.

Kingsbury, of course, was merely the first of many who would shatter records.

When he left, he owned 39 school records, 13 Big 12 Conference records and seven NCAA Football Bowl Subdivision records. His final tally read: 1,229 of 1,881 passes completed for 12,423 yards and 95 touchdowns.

Still, Kingsbury's relationship with his alma mater is complicated.

He violated a tried-and-true mantra: Don't ever work for family. It's awkward firing your own son.

That's what Kliff did, returning home to take

Kliff Kingsbury

over the head coaching job in 2013.

It wasn't a good fit, though this Hollywood handsome coach undoubtedly diversified the fan base with more women suddenly taking interest in the football program.

Kliff had built a resume on tutoring quarterbacks. He had gained a reputation as a great offensive mind after having made good quarterbacks out of Case Keenum at Houston, as well as Johnny Manziel – Johnny Football – who won the Heisman Trophy at Texas A&M.

Word in the industry was that Kliff was a quarterback whisperer.

Yet Kliff racked up a less than stellar 35-39 record in six seasons at Tech, never finishing above fifth in the conference.

Now, of course, we're all indebted to him for bringing Patrick Mahomes to campus.

Patrick Mahomes, the Wizard From Whitehouse

THE MOST ACCLAIMED FOOTBALL player in Texas Tech history is this two-time Super Bowl champion and NFL MVP.

What a story. Despite having the size (6-foot-3), arm strength, athleticism and pedigree (his father Pat had been an MLB pitcher), Patrick Lavon Mahomes II was lightly recruited out of Whitehouse, a suburb of Tyler. He was not seen as a particularly good prospect, stemming from his desire to also play baseball.

In high school, Mahomes took over as starting quarterback as a junior, passing 3,839 yards and scoring 46 touchdowns. That garnered the attention of a few schools. Among them was Texas Tech. Kliff Kingsbury offered a scholarship to Mahomes, 10 months before he could actually sign a letter of intent. Mahomes committed on the spot to sign it when he could. Only Houston and Rice were other

Patrick Mahomes

known suitors.

The future star stepped into a quarterback room in 2014 with two other future NFL players. Baker Mayfield and Davis Webb were already on the roster with experience and notches on their belt.

Mayfield elected to transfer to Oklahoma. Webb stayed another year, but he, too, transferred after the 2014 season, beginning the start of the Mahomes rein.

In two-and-a-half seasons, Mahomes passed for 11,252 yards and 93 touchdowns. As a junior in 2016, his final season of college football, Mahomes led the country with 5,052 yards. He also made 41 touchdowns.

Against Oklahoma that season, he had 734 yards passing and five touchdowns in outdueling but losing to Baker Mayfield – Tech's 59 points not enough to win. Yet, the 734 yards *tied* the FBS record for a game. The total did snap Texas Tech and

Mahomes by the numbers

22 Rushing TDs, second all-time in school history.

88 Pass attempts in a game, a single-game record.

93 TDs, third in Texas Tech history.

857 Completions, third in Texas Tech history.

5,052 Passing yards in 2016. No. 1 in nation.

11,252 Passing yards in 2 1/2 seasons, third in Texas Tech history.

Big 12 single-game records for passing.

His 819 yards of total offense in that game, though, were Big 12 and FBS records.

Insane.

As far as other Tech records, Mahomes set marks in a single game for pass attempts (88), completions (52), and most plays. Amazingly, his 5,052 passing yards was good for only fourth all-time in the program's history.

His career passing yards ranked third all-time at Tech. So, too, were his touchdown totals, attempts (1,349) and completions (857). His 22 rushing touchdowns ranked second for a quarterback.

With the Chiefs, he made his mark as the veritable face of the NFL. And that face is associated with Texas Tech because he has promoted the school like he does his Whataburger franchises in Kansas City.

"I'm a huge fan," Tech coach Joey McGuire said. "We've talked. It's really good to have him on our side."

McGuire said Mahomes is willing to promote the school any time he's asked.

"He's like, 'I've got you, Coach.' So he's really proud to be a Red Raider; I know that."

The Runners

BEFORE THE ARRIVAL of Mike Leach's "Air Raid" offensive assault, Texas Tech controlled games on the ground, producing some of the best running backs in the country over the years.

Byron Hanspard (1994-96), Texas Tech's top gainer in career rushing yards with 4,219. He also holds the school record for most yards in a game (287 vs. Baylor, 1996) and a season (2,084 in 1996).

James Gray, (1986-89). A devourer of football turf, Gray rushed for 4,066 yards and a school-record 52 career touchdowns.

Ricky Williams (1997-2001) gained the third-most rushing yards in school history, 3,661 yards and 36 rushing touchdowns as a Red Raider.

Donny Anderson (1963-65), the "Golden Palomino," had NFL scouts salivating while collecting more than 3,600 yards and 28 touchdowns in three seasons from 1963-65 as a more than capable runner and pass catcher out of the backfield.

Bam Morris (1991-93), a product of little Cooper, Texas, rushed for 3,545 and 37 touchdowns from 1991-93 before heading off to a productive, albeit short, career with the Pittsburgh Steelers.

The Passers

MIKE LEACH'S OFFENSES were a quarterback's best friend. If you played the position at Texas during that time, you were headed to the top of NCAA stats boards.

The most notable gun slinger was Graham Harrell, who with wide receiver Michael Crabtree, lit up scoreboards and harassed defenses

Texas Tech career passing leaders

Name	Years	Yards	TDs
Graham Harrell*	(2005-08)	15,793	134
Kliff Kingsbury*	(1999-02)	12,429	95
Patrick Mahomes	(2014-16)	11,252	93
Seth Doege	(2009-12)	8,636	69
Robert Hall	(1990-93)	7,908	48
Taylor Potts*	(2007-10)	7,835	62
Zebbie Lethridge	(1994-97)	6,789	42
Billy Joe Tolliver	(1985-88)	6,756	38
BJ Symons*	(2000-03)	6,378	59
Davis Webb	(2013-15)	5,557	46

*Played for Mike Leach

Patrick Mahomes

from 2005-08. His 15,793 career passing yards is fourth all-time.

Kliff Kingsbury, who played three seasons under Leach, is 33rd in career passing yards.

Six of the top 10 passers in school history played for Leach or his protégé, Kingsbury.

From Pampa to Canton

ONE PLAYER FROM TEXAS TECH has been elected to Canton's Pro Football Hall of Fame.

He is Pampa's Zach Thomas, who was selected in 2023.

Thomas, a five-time first team All-Pro selection, was one of nine NFL greats selected for induction, joining, among others, Ronde Barber, Chuck Howley, Joe Klecko, Darrelle Revis, and DeMarcus Ware.

Over his 13 NFL seasons, including 12 in Miami and one with the Dallas Cowboys, Thomas was one of the league's most consistent players.

Always considered too small for the position, Thomas silenced doubters with 10 seasons of at least 100 tackles, eventually finishing his career with 1,734 stops, the fifth-highest total in league history. Seven times he was selected to the Pro Bowl and twice NFL Linebacker of the Year.

His career at Texas Tech was among the best in school history.

Thomas, a College Football Hall of Famer, was a two-time first team All-American, including a unanimous choice in 1995. He led the Red Raiders to a share of the 1994 Southwest Conference title and three consecutive bowl games, including the 1995 Cotton Bowl disaster against Southern California.

Zach Thomas

Thomas ranks fifth all-time in school history with 390 career tackles, and he holds the school record with seven career fumble recoveries.

He was also the key player in one of the most memorable plays in Texas Tech history.

With the 1995 game against Texas A&M tied in the final minute, Thomas stepped in front of a pass intended for Aggies receiver Albert Connell and returned it 23 yards for a touchdown with 30 seconds remaining to allow the Red Raiders to knock off the No. 8 Aggies, 14-7.

The victory snapped A&M's string of 29 consecutive SWC games without a loss, dating to Dec. 1, 1990.

Thomas had played a hunch and drifted into pass coverage. Aggies QB Corey Pullig never saw him.

"I don't know why I did it. Something just told me to get over there," said Thomas, who, for the first time all day, drifted into double-coverage on a slant across the middle. "I read the quarterback's eyes and cut the ball off. I saw the end zone and just ran for the line."

Said coach Spike Dykes: "What's more of a fitting ending than that? It was a great play by a great player. He guessed right and he robbed a pattern."

The rest of the story went like this:

Thomas wasn't even supposed to play because he was sick with the "kissing disease," mononucleosis.

"He told me there was no way he would miss the game with Texas A&M, no matter how he felt," Thomas' father Steve told the *Avalanche-Journal*.

After the victory, "Spike said he wanted to kiss him," the player's father went on. But "when he took off Zach's helmet and saw the sores on his mouth from mono, Spike said, 'On second thought, maybe not.'"

Five Legendary Teams

2008

THE SEASON IS WIDELY considered one of Texas Tech's most historic. Under coach Mike Leach, the Red Raiders finished 11-2 record and won the Big 12 South division. Led by quarterback Graham Harrell, who finished fourth in the Heisman Trophy voting, and wide receiver Michael Crabtree, who finished fifth, Texas Tech averaged 43.8 points per game.

Aug. 30	E. Washington	W, 49-24
Sept. 6	at Nevada	W, 35-19
Sept. 13	SMU	W, 43-7
Oct. 4	at Kansas State	W, 58-28
Oct. 11	Nebraska	W, 37-31
Oct. 18	at Texas A&M	W, 43-25
Oct. 25	at Kansas	W, 63-21
Nov. 1	Texas	W, 39-33
Nov. 8	Oklahoma State	W, 56-20
Nov. 22	at Oklahoma	L, 65-21
Nov. 29	Baylor	W, 35-28
Jan. 2	Ole Miss	L, 47-37

The Red Raiders rose to a program-high No. 2 in the country after a victory over Oklahoma State. The most spell binding of 11 consecutive victories to start the season was a 39-33 triumph over No. 1 Texas at AT&T Jones Stadium in Lubbock. Harrell hit Crabtree in the last 10 seconds along the sideline. Crabtree spun out of a tackle, and sprinted into the end zone for the winning score.

Tech earned a spot in the Cotton Bowl, a loss to Ole Miss at AT&T Stadium in Arlington.

1973

TEXAS TECH UNDER COACH Jim Carlen was the nation's surprise team that year. The Red Raiders' only blemish was its loss to Southwest Conference champion Texas. Tech finished 11-1 with a victory over Tennessee in the Gator Bowl to finish No. 11 in the AP poll.

The guy who made it all go: Quarterback Joe Barnes, winner

Sept. 15	Utah	W, 29-22
Sept. 22	New Mexico	W, 41-17
Sept. 29	at Texas	L, 28-12
Oct. 6	at Oklahoma State	W, 20-7
Oct. 13	Texas A&M	W, 28-16
Oct. 20	at Arizona	W, 31-17
Oct. 27	SMU	W, 31-14
Nov. 3	Rice	W, 19-6
Nov. 10	at TCU	W, 24-10
Nov. 17	Baylor	W, 55-24
Nov. 24	at Arkansas	W, 24-17
Dec. 29	Tennessee	W, 28-19

of the Kern Tips Memorial Award, then presented annually to the top senior player in the Southwest Conference.

"Barnes was the difference," said Arkansas coach Frank Broyles after the Raiders beat the Razorbacks for the first time in six seasons, 24-17 in Little Rock. "He made the big plays every time. He's a great quarterback, certainly all-conference in this league. His ability to make you miss him is almost uncanny."

As the most valuable player in the Gator Bowl, Barnes had 231 yards combined rushing and passing, including two TDs passing and one rushing.

1953

By winning 11 games in 1953, the Red Raiders boosted their argument for inclusion in the Southwest Conference. Tech went 11-1 as Border Conference champions in a season that ended with an appearance in the Gator Bowl against Auburn. Tech finished 12th in the AP Poll.

Bobby Cavazos, an honorable mention all-America running back in 1951 and a second-team All-American in 1953, was one of the most decorated players in Texas Tech history. He played on a team that succeeded at one of the most pivotal moments in school history.

"You are the envy of all other college teams," booster Amon G. Carter, the first president of the school's board of regents, wrote coach Dewitt Weaver. "You should have been selected for the Sugar Bowl …

Sept. 19	West Texas State	W, 40-14
Sept. 26	at UTEP	W, 27-6
Oct. 3	at Oklahoma State	W, 27-13
Oct. 10	Texas A&M	L, 27-14
Oct. 17	Pacific	W, 34-7
Oct. 25	New Mexico State	W, 71-0
Oct. 31	at Mississippi St.	W, 27-20
Nov. 7	Arizona	W, 52-27
Nov. 14	at Tulsa	W, 49-7
Nov. 21	at Houston	W, 41-21
Nov. 28	Hardin-Simmons	W, 46-12
Jan. 1	Auburn	W, 35-13

and Tech should be in the Southwest Conference. So, keep up the good work, and if the college authorities do not recognize you, the public in Texas will demand it."

In the Gator Bowl, Cavazos, the game's most valuable player, ran for 141 yards on just 13 carries and scored three touchdowns, his last one for 59 yards, then a Gator Bowl record.

In 1953, he was chosen "Mr. Texas Tech University."

"He was the most popular man," former teammate and roommate Jack Kirkpatrick told the *Avlanche-Journal*. "Everybody liked him." In 1953, Cavazos was named "Mr. Texas Tech University."

On the trip back to Lubbock, Cavazos was met at the airport during a stopover in Fort Worth by his brother, Lt. Richard Cavazos, later a four-star general after whom Fort Hood in Killeen, the nation's biggest Army base, was renamed. His other brother, Lauro, became president of Texas Tech before serving as secretary of education under presidents Ronald Reagan and George H.W. Bush.

Bobby Cavazos

All were sons of a King Ranch foreman.

Cavazos was selected in the first round of the NFL Draft by the Chicago Cardinals in 1954, but he

Sept. 11	Colorado	W, 24-7
Sept. 25	at New Mexico	W, 20-16
Oct. 9	at Texas A&M	W, 27-16
Oct. 16	at Rice	W, 37-13
Oct. 23	Arizona	W, 52-27
Oct. 30	Texas	W, 31-28
Nov. 6	at TCU	W, 14-10
Nov. 13	SMU	W, 34-7
Nov. 20	Houston	L, 27-19
Nov. 27	at Arkansas	W, 30-7
Dec. 4	Baylor	W, 24-21
Dec. 31	Nebraska	L, 27-24

never played in a regular-season game after a serious shoulder injury in his first preseason game. He headed back to the King Ranch in Kingsville.

Aside from ranching, Cavazos also became a published author, writing *The Cowboy from the Wild Horse Desert: A Story of the King Ranch*, and *The Cowboy from the Wild Horse Desert book two:* The Saga Continues.

"There was a lot of guys that (football) was the only thing they had going for them," Cavazos said, according to the Lubbock paper's obituary. "But I knew that I had my job back there with dad on the King Ranch, because I had worked for him every summer." He died in 2013 at 82.

1976

Like 1973, Texas Tech surprised and surpassed the expectations by going 10-2 under coach Steve Sloan and claiming a share of the Southwest Conference championship and an appearance in the Bluebonnet Bowl.

Rodney Allison, the conference's MVP, was a big reason why.

Rodney Allison

Allison passed for 1,651 yards (second in the SWC) and 10 touchdowns (third in the SWC) and rushed for more than 600 yards and 10 more touchdowns (second in the SWC).

Tech was 8-0 and ranked fifth nationally before No. 9 Houston defeated the Red Raiders 27-19 on Nov. 20 at AT&T Jones Stadium. The Red Raiders rallied from 27-5 and were advancing again when Allison threw an interception deep in Houston territory.

Houston and coach Bill Yoeman finished fourth

in the country after beating then-No. 4 Maryland in the Cotton Bowl.

"All those great things happened throughout my career," Allison told the *Avalanche-Journal*. "But that one thing that still haunts me to this day was that interception against Houston in '76."

1938

The Red Raiders, led by running back Elmer Tarbox, had their best football season to that point, winning 10 consecutive games before being upset by St. Mary's of California in the Cotton Bowl.

Nonetheless, Tech won the Border Conference championship under coach Pete Cawthon, who coached from 1931-40.

The Cotton Bowl was ugly. The Red Raiders committed eight turnovers, in-

Sept. 17	Montana State	W, 35-0
Sept. 24	Wyoming	W, 39-0
Sept. 30	at Duquesne	W, 7-6
Oct. 8	at Oklahoma City	W, 60-0
Oct. 15	at Montana	W, 19-13
Oct. 22	at UTEP	W, 14-7
Nov. 5	Loyola New Orleans	W, 55-0
Nov. 11	Gonzaga	W, 7-0
Nov. 19	at New Mexico	W, 17-7
Nov. 26	Marquette	W, 21-2
Jan. 2	Saint Mary's (CA)	L, 20-13

cluding five interceptions and got down 20-0.

Tech, however, scored twice in the fourth quarter on TD catches by Tarbox and E.J. McKnight from quarterback Gene Barnett. Tech was driving to tie the game late but stalled at St. Mary's 15-yard line in what was considered a monumental upset.

"It would have been a crime for us to have beaten them," said Texas Tech coach Pete Cawthon.

Legendary coaches

Mike "The Pirate" Leach (2000-09)

LEACH WAS THE STRANGEST, most successful football coach in Tech history.

The Pirate was as likely to talk your ear off about football as he was about the wisdom of eloping rather than spending tens of thousands of dollars on a wedding party your parents want to throw.

Mike Leach

Leach, who suffered a fatal heart attack in 2022 at 61, revolutionized Texas Tech football. Known for his innovative "Air Raid" offense, Leach led the Red Raiders to unprecedented success. He compiled an 84-43 record and guided Texas Tech to 10 bowl appearances, including a trip to the 2008 Cotton Bowl. Leach's offensive approach helped produce high-scoring games and numerous passing records.

Leach stories are countless.

Lincoln Riley, his one-time assistant who went on to head coaching jobs at Oklahoma and USC, remembered a phone call Leach took on his cell phone while in the coaches' office. Riley said he was minding his own business, though he couldn't help but overhear some of the conversation. Twenty minutes or a half hour goes by and the call drops. Leach redials. "Sorry," he says, "we must have been disconnected."

Another hour goes by and Leach hangs up. "Who was it," Riley asks? "Oh, they had the wrong number."

As Oklahoma's offensive coordinator in 1999, Leach pulled off a strategic deception worthy of the Greeks' fabled Trojan Horse to undermine an entrenched enemy. The Red River Rivalry is serious business and Leach worked to improve his team's odds by instructing a player to "accidentally" drop a play sheet on the University of Texas sideline. It was found by a UT staffer and considered legitimate.

The plays were believable. But they were not the ones OU would run that game or at least not in that order. OU began the game 17-0 until Texas realized the ruse and stopped following the fake play sheet. UT would go on to win 38-28.

Year	Record	Big 12	Final AP
2000	7-6	3-5	
2001	7-5	4-4	
2002	9-5	5-3	
2003	8-5	4-4	
2004	8-4	5-3	18
2005	9-3	6-2	20
2006	8-5	4-4	
2007	9-4	4-4	22
2008	11-2	7-1	12
2009	8-4	5-3	21

Genius?

Perhaps *mad* genius fits best.

In a 2005 interview with the *New York Times,* Leach, known for his love of pirates, wondered about the Corps of Cadets at Texas A&M.

"How come (Aggies) get to pretend they are soldiers? ... I ought to have 'Mike's Pirate School.' The freshmen, all they get is the bandanna. When you're a senior, you get the sword and skull and crossbones. For homework, we'll work pirate maneuvers and stuff like that."

Leach had a home in Key West. The locals often spotted him there. The bartenders felt as ambivalent about him as the administration at Texas Tech.

At the Green Parrot, a bar there, is a sign on the wall:

"Key West Pirate and Torture Museum
303 Simonton St.
(Next to the post office)"

That irony might hit a little close to home as he found himself embroiled in controversy in 2009 for his handling of wide receiver Adam James, who was suffering from concussion symptoms. James said he couldn't practice and as an alternative to practice, Leach reportedly forced him to sit by himself in a dark room. Tech fired the coach in the aftermath.

Lots of fans are still not over that. Leach likely went to his grave still pissed at the school's administration.

Fans witnessed the school's biggest victory in its history under Leach in 2008, a 39-33 victory over No. 1 Texas. Graham Harrell's pass to Michael

Crabtree etched in memories for a long time.

As for Leach, he was eventually hired at Washington State, where he had similar success.

"As a head coach, you're on two lists," Leach told the *Seattle Times*. "You're the guy that might get fired, or you're the guy who might go somewhere. Given the two lists, I guess that's the one to be on."

At the time of his death, Leach was head coach at Mississippi State, where he spent three seasons.

Following his firing at Tech, Leach spewed vitriol, going so far as to hire a political consultant to lobby the Texas Legislature for a bill allowing public universities to be sued. The effort failed.

In the end, Tech got the last word. The Red Raiders beat Mississippi State 34-7 in the Liberty Bowl in 2021.

"I guess the Red Raider gets the Pirate after all," said Tech coach Sonny Cumbie, who had been coached by Leach when a player in Lubbock.

The year following his death, the university tried to make amends for the acrimonious way the two parted company by inducting Leach into Texas Tech's Ring of Honor.

Spike Dykes (1986-1999)

SPIKE DYKES' TEXAS TECH football teams won more than seven games only twice in his 13 full seasons at head coach, yet going to seven bowl games during that time represented progress.

Spike Dykes

There's another reason Dykes is on Tech's Mount Rushmore for coaches:

His teams beat rivals Texas and Texas A&M six times apiece.

He was also a reporter's dream, always ready with a quip or witticism, sometimes aiming at himself with a self-deprecating humor that endeared him to the masses.

"They whipped us like a tied-up goat," he said after a forgettable, well, whipping.

When Dykes retired after the 1999 season, he had a record 82 victories.

Dykes was a longtime Texas high school football coach when he joined the staff as an assistant on Jerry Moore's staff in 1984. He was promoted to head coach after David McWilliams' departure before the Independence Bowl in 1986.

He was a three-time Southwest Conference coach of the year and the Big 12 coach of the year in the conference's first season.

Year	Record	SWC/Big 12	Final AP
1986	0-1 (coached Independence Bowl)		
1987	6-4-1	3-3-1	
1988	5-6	4-3	
1989	9-3	5-3	19
1990	4-7	3-5	
1991	6-5	5-3	
1992	5-6	4-3	
1994	6-6	5-2	
1995	9-3	5-2	23
1996	7-5	5-3*	
1997	6-5	5-3	
1998	7-5	4-4	22
1999	6-5	5-3	

*First year of Big 12

"I'll always be very appreciative of Texas Tech for giving me a chance," Dykes said some years after his retirement. "I'm an old high school coach and woke up one day and T. Jones was athletic director and Dr. [Lauro] Cavazos was our president. They offered me a job, so I took it. It was a lot of fun, a great ride."

Dykes was born in a Lubbock hospital across the street from the Texas Tech campus.

He paid his dues as a high school coach from 1959-71 at Eastland, Ballinger, San Angelo Central, Coahoma, Belton, Big Spring and Alice.

Darrell Royal hired him as an assistant at Texas from 1971-76 and an assistant at New Mexico and Mississippi State.

He came back to West Texas to be head coach at Midland Lee from 1980-83, reaching a 1983 state championship game with Tyrone Thurman among his star players.

His 1989 Tech team was memorable.

It was picked to finish sixth in the SWC but went 9-3 with Jamie Gill at quarterback and star running back James Gray as the primary ball carrier.

Victories included triumphs over No. 20 Arizona, No. 19 Texas A&M, No. 22 Texas, and No. 20 Duke in the All-American Bowl.

Gill beat the Aggies with a last-minute touchdown pass to Travis Price and did the same to the Longhorns in Austin with a fourth-quarter TD pass to Anthony Manyweather, who came to Lubbock from California, asking Dykes for a chance to play. Both were on third-and-26 situations.

Twilight Zone stuff.

Mayweather was looking for a place to study engineering and play football. He had enough money to get to Lubbock, but not enough to get back to the Coast, Dykes said.

"I think it says something about the character of this team," Dykes remarked about its memorable fourth-quarter comebacks. "When some teams start folding their tent, these guys seem to gain confidence."

"He was a true legend to me," said Montae Reagor, who spoke to the *Avalanche-Journal* after Dykes' death in 2017. "He was more than a coach; he was a father figure. I don't care how hard he coached us, at the end of the day, we knew he loved us from the bottom of his heart.

"There aren't many like Spike. He's just a gracious, loving man. I will never forget him."

Jim Carlen (1970-1974)

CARLEN BROUGHT STABILITY and success to the Texas Tech football program. Under his leadership, the Red Raiders had a 37-20-2 record. Carlen led Texas Tech to three bowl appearances, including a victory in the Gator Bowl in 1973.

Year	Record	SWC	Final AP
1970	8-4	5-2	
1971	4-7	2-5	
1972	8-4	4-3	
1973	11-1	6-1	11
1974	6-4-2	3-4	

Carlen, who was born in Cookeville, Tennessee, took over for former coach J.T. King in 1970. Tech had made just two bowl appearances in the previous 15 seasons before Carlen's arrival, but he led the program to bowls in four of his five seasons.

Three times Carlen, who neither smoked nor drank and didn't tolerate anyone else who did, was Southwest Conference coach of the year. In 1973, a season only marked by a loss to SWC champion Texas, Carlen was selected national coach of the year. The Red Raiders finished ranked No. 11 by the AP.

"It wasn't really until I got out of school that I realized what kind of coach he was," said Joe Barnes, who led the 1973 team as quarterback, telling the *Lubbock Avalanche-Journal*at the time of the coach's death in 2012: "He would keep [players] at arm's length but he would go to bat for all his players."

Said Don Rives, an All-Southwest Conference performer who played for Carlen from 1970-72: "One of my fondest memories was his willingness to share his faith. …. He was a great Christian man with great values, and he passed them on to all of us."

DeWitt Weaver (1951-60)

WHEN TULSA ASSISTANT COACH DeWitt Weaver told his boss, head coach Buddy Brothers, he was leaving to become head coach at Texas Tech, Brothers told him: "You're crazy."

Tech had yet to establish relevancy in its football program and the worksite was "all the way out there" in Lubbock.

Weaver left a giant footprint, taking Tech football – and athletics – from relative obscurity to relevance.

No one to that point had done more for Tech athletics than Weaver, who was also athletic director and successfully led the push for the Red Raiders' inclusion in the Southwest Conference.

During his 10 seasons, Tech won four Border Conference championships and was runner-up another. Tech played in three bowl games. Five sections were added to the stadium, taking the seating capacity from 19,000 to 41,000.

Year	Record	Border	Final AP
1951	7-4	4-0	
1952	3-7-1	2-1-1	
1953	11-1	5-0	12
1954	7-2-1	4-0	
1955	7-3-1	3-0-1	
1956	2-7-1	*	
1957	2-8	*	
1958	3-7		
1959	4-6	*	
1960	3-6-1	1-5-1	

*Played as independent while awaiting entrance to SWC

Weaver was at the helm of the athletics office on Texas Tech sports' most important day, May 12, 1956, the day Southwest Conference members admittrf the Red Raiders.

"It was a team triumph," the *Avalanche-Journal* recounted, " ... but it was Weaver who engineered the entire thing. Credit belongs to him."

Pete Cawthon (1930-40)

TEXAS TECH WAS INTRODUCED to Cawthon in 1925. He was the coach at Austin College, which tied with Tech 3-3 that season. Five years later, he was coaching in Lubbock.

Cawthon's tenure in Lubbock was ground-breaking. In 1932, he constructed the nation's highest-scoring offense. He also led the Matadors to the Sun Bowl and Cotton Bowl in 1938 and 1939.

Year	Record	Border	Final AP
1932	10-2	2-0	
1933	8-1	1-0	
1934	7-2-1	1-0	
1935	5-3-2	0-1	
1936	5-4-1	—	
1937	8-4	3-0	
1938	10-1	2-0	
1939	5-5-1	2-1	11
1940	9-1-1	0-1	

In 1934, Cawthon was also something of a marketing maven, outfitting his team in red satin uniforms and worked to build its reputation beyond Texas by scheduling games across the nation.

Sports writers began referring to the Matadors as the "Red Raiders."

In 1937, Tech became the nation's first college

football team to fly to a road game when Cawthon, backed by the Tech athletic council, chartered a DC-3 to fly from Meacham Field in Fort Worth to Michigan to play the University of Detroit.

During his tenure, Cawthon went 78-32-6. His nearly 68 percent win percentage remains a program record.

Controversy enveloped him as well. His use of ineligible players, Bobby Holmes and Forrest Jones, caused Tech to be banished from the Border Conference for two years.

"I don't know anything about it," Cawthon insisted to reporters.

He then ran into trouble with his bosses, who were working to get Tech in the Southwest Conference.

After filling his schedule in 1940 without a single Texas team on it, Tech administrators asked for his resignation. Cawthon obliged.

Of particular interest to the administration was seeing Hardin-Simmons back on the schedule.

The Dallas Morning News commented on the kerfuffle by saying: "The likable Cawthon can be a very stubborn man. For some reason he didn't want his teams to play those of H-SU again; set his mind against such contests and refused to be swayed even though he knew – and he has known for months – that me might be asked to resign if he didn't see eye to eye with the [athletic] council on the subject."

J.T. King (1961-69)

HOW IS A COACH with a 44-45-3 record over seasons considered legendary?

King inherited a program that had run into a ditch. The Red Raiders had gone 14-34-2 in five consecutive losing seasons before he took over from DeWitt Weaver.

King also marshaled the school into the teeth of the big boys of the Southwest Conference.

The reasons

Year	Record	SWC	Final AP
1961	4-6	2-5	
1962	1-9	0-7	
1963	5-5	2-5	
1964	6-4-1	3-3-1	
1965	8-3	5-2	
1966	4-6	2-5	
1967	6-4	5-2	
1968	5-3	4-3	
1969	5-5	4-3	

for the early struggles were of no concern to alumni and fans. King encountered fan opposition from the start because of the losses.

Still, Tech finished .500 or better in six of his last seven seasons, including bowl teams in 1964 and 1965. And coaches look adept when they have players like Donny Anderson.

The Red Raiders under King orchestrated what was considered the upset of the year by beating Arkansas in 1966 to knock the Razorbacks out of the Cotton Bowl. And in 1967, quarterback John Scovell rushed for 175 yards in a historic 19-13 upset of Texas in Austin.

The victory was Tech's first over Texas in eight tries in the Southwest Conference.

The smartest guys in the room said it was a fluke, but Tech came back the next year to do it again in Lubbock.

A new day was upon the Raiders football program.

"It was a moment of grudging satisfaction for J.T. King, the Raider boss who once played guard for the Longhorns and later served his alma mater as an assistant coach," wrote the *Dallas Morning*

News. "There was no flukiness to this victory, for Tech came into this early SWC showdown with a masterful game plan and in Scovell had an operator to carry it out."

Darrell Royal, the Texas coach, said years afterward that Scovell's triple-option maneuvering left the Longhorns in a "frazzle," accelerating his team's switch to the wishbone offense.

King's very best moves at Tech occurred while he was athletic director from 1970-78.

He first hired Jim Carlen as his replacement in 1970 and Steve Sloan in 1975. Both brought unprecedented success for Tech in the Southwest Conference.

Five Legendary Games

Nov. 1, 2008
No. 7 Texas Tech 39, No. 1 Texas 33

The Red Raiders' march to college football relevance in the modern age intersected with a state archrival UT. Down 33-32 with just 1:29 to play, Tech's high-octane offense led by Graham Harrell, recently named a nominee for the National Football Foundation Hall of Fame, and Michael Crabtree pulled off what many consider the epitome of Red Raider football. Despite a broken ankle, Crabtree grabbed the pass and spun into the end zone, capping a glorious six-play drive and the biggest victory in school history.

Oct. 7, 1995
Texas Tech 14, No. 8 Texas A&M 7

With the game tied 7-7 and just 45 seconds left, linebacker Zach Thomas stepped in front of Corey Pullig's pass intended for A&M receiver Albert Connell and returned it 23 yards for a touchdown with 30 seconds remaining, snapping the Aggies' string of 29 consecutive SWC games without a loss, dating to Dec. 1, 1990.

Oct. 5, 2002
Texas Tech 48, Texas A&M 47 (OT)

Playing at Kyle Field, the Aggies jumped to an 18-point fourth-quarter lead. Red Raiders QB Kliff Kingsbury, however, led his team to 17 points in the final quarter to send the game to overtime. A&M scored a touchdown to open overtime, but kicker John Pierson missed his second extra-point attempt of the game. On the ensuing possession, Kingsbury hit Nehemiah Glover for a touchdown and Robert Treece's extra-point try was good giving Texas Tech an inconceivable victory over the miserable Aggies.

Oct. 30, 1976
No. 6 Texas Tech 31, Texas 28

Down 28-24 Tech quarterback Rodney Allison rallied his team from behind on the final drive, including a scramble for 22 yards on a pivotal third-and-7. Billy Taylor scored from the 1-yard line to put Tech up and defensive coordinator Bill Parcells' defensive unit held in the closing moments.

Nov. 19, 2005
No. 21 Texas Tech 23, Oklahoma 21

Texas Tech QB Cody Hodges led Texas Tech on one of the most controversial drives in Big 12 history. Three of the drive's 13 plays were reviewed by game officials, including Taurean Henderson's 3-yard-run-and-desperation-dive   game-winner. Triumph stamped Texas Tech's ticket to the Cotton Bowl, where a wacky, knuckleball field goal – it fluttered and danced though the air with no spin like a Charlie Hough pitch – got them beat by Alabama.

NFL Honor Roll

SOME OTHER GUYS NOT NAMED Patrick Mahomes or Zach Thomas.

Danny Amendola (2004-07 at Tech), like Wes Welker, wasn't a player who quickly impressed NFL scouts, but he ended up turning in a productive 13-year career with five teams, including the New England Patriots, with whom he won two of three Super Bowls played in.

Donny Anderson (1963-65), a first-round pick, signed for an unprecedented $700,000 with the Green Bay Packers, eclipsing the $400,000 the New York Jets had paid Joe Namath. That's a whopping $6.5 million in 2023 dollars. One of his best games was the renowned Ice Bowl against the Dallas Cowboys, perhaps the most famous game in NFL history. With the temperature at minus-13 (minus-46 with the wind chill), Anderson handled the ball 30 times, including punts, and shined in the 68-yard final drive by catching three passes for 27 yards. He also picked up two pivotal first downs.

Maury Buford (1978-81) enjoyed a nine-year career as a punter with three teams, including the dominant 1985 Chicago Bears.

Marcus Coleman (1992-95) was a good NFL defensive back, collecting 25 interceptions over an 11-year career with the New York Jets, Houston Texas, and Dallas Cowboys.

Michael Crabtree (2007-08), one of the school's best receivers, was drafted 10th overall in 2009. During 11 seasons, he had 637 catches for 7,499 yards and 54 touchdowns. In San Francisco's 2012 Super Bowl season, Crabtree had 85 receptions for more than 1,100 yards.

Michael Crabtree

Lin Elliott (1989-91) set a Dallas Cowboys rookie record with 24 field goals in 1992. His 119 points was also a rookie record while ranking fourth in the NFL. He was part of the Cowboys' Super Bowl XXVII championship team.

"The Beast," E.J. Holub (1958-60), was born in Schulenburg and raised in Lubbock. He was drafted high by both the Dallas Cowboys of the NFL and the Dallas Texans of the AFL. He chose to go the way of the AFL and Lamar Hunt, who eventually moved the team to Kansas City and changed the name to the Chiefs. Holub started 113 games combined for the Texans and Chiefs over a nine-year pro football career. He is distinguished as the only player to start on both offense and defense in the history of the Super Bowl. In Super Bowl I, he started at linebacker. He was the starting center in

E.J. Holub

the Chiefs' Super Bowl IV appearance.

Defensive back Curtis Jordan (1972-75) played in 145 games from 1976-86 with the Tampa Bay Buccaneers and Washington Commanders, with whom he played in two Super Bowls, one a winner.

Bam Morris (1991-93), a running back, played in Super Bowl XXX with Pittsburgh as part of seven-year career with four teams.

Sammy Morris (1996-99), a running back, played 12 seasons for the Buffalo Bills, Miami Dolphins, New England Patriots, and the Dallas Cowboys. He played in the Super Bowl with New England in 2008.

Dave Parks (1961-63) at one time held the school records for career receptions (80), single-season receptions (32), single-game receptions (eight), and single game receiving yards (132 vs Kansas State in 1963). The San Francisco 49ers made Parks the No. 1 pick in the 1964 draft, to this day the only Texas Tech player to be drafted first over-all. Parks was an immediate hit, grabbing All-Pro honors in 1965-66 and the Pro Bowl in 1967. Parks closed his career with Pro Football Hall of Fame credentials, with more than 5,600 yards and 44 touchdowns. Some go so far as to say his omission from Canton is a sports crime.

Timmy Smith (1982-86) had one shining moment as a rookie running back for Washington. Smith, born and raised in Hobbs, New Mexico, set a Super Bowl rushing record in his first career start with 204 yards and two touchdowns in a 42-10 victory over Denver.

Billy Joe Tolliver

Billy Joe Tolliver (1985-88) had arm strength, arm strength, and more arm strength, which he used to throw passes in 10 NFL seasons. Over the course of that time, Big Opie passed for 10,760 yards and 59 touchdowns for

81

the San Diego Chargers, Atlanta Falcons, Houston Oilers, Kansas City Chiefs and New Orleans Saints.

Bake Turner (1959-61) was a 1,000-yard receiver for the Jets in 1963, one part of a career that also included a Super Bowl victory with Joe Namath in 1969.

Louis Vasquez (2005-08) was a Super Bowl champion as an offensive lineman for the Denver Broncos in 2016. He played in more than 100 games over seven seasons with San Diego and Denver.

Joe Walter (1981-84) spent 12 seasons with the Cincinnati Bengals as a tackle. He played in the Super Bowl in 1989.

Ted Watts (1978-80), a defensive back, had five interceptions and three fumble recoveries over six seasons with the Oakland/Los Angeles Raiders and New York Giants. He played in Super Bowl XVIII in 1984.